MICROCOSMS

POETRY ON PERSPECTIVE

R J O'Connor

BookLeaf Publishing

India | USA | UK

Presentation by *BookLeaf Publishing*

Web: www.bookleafpub.com

E-mail: info@bookleafpub.com

ISBN : 9789358361773

First edition 2021

DEDICATION

To Jo, who enjoys microcosms as much as I do.

PREFACE

I hope that you, reader, as much as I do, stop to look at the light reflecting on a puddle, the flight of bees around a lavender plant, or the gills on a mushroom beneath a tree. These poems are just snippets of perspective: a (hopefully) new way of looking at something that is often dismissed or overlooked. Their style changes from poem to poem, in an attempt to reflect the different subject matter, and some are longer than others. I hope that you appreciate the microcosm that is this book.

Thank you for reading.

1.

here we stay, we undeserving,

in the cage of our preserving.

here we're captured, sun-light raptured,

'waiting violence of release.

see our kingdom caught and kenneled;

see our folk and forces funnelled:

gaze upon us, dark colossus —

by your parting, give us peace.

\- A ROCK-POOL

2.

i am clinging in this tempest
to the rock beneath me, helpless,
and from moment unto moment,
facing desperately the test:
certain death if courage fails me,
or the unknown end of journey.
there's serenity in holding on
and hoping for the best.

- BEE ON THE WINDSCREEN

there's been murder in the meadow:

one has killed their fickle fellow,

sending safety to the shadows

and defiling the dirt.

accusation ebbs around it;

careful, cautious for the culprit.

all is fearful and fervent:

sanctity is slaughter-girt.

tart and telling is it's tasting

as the wretch is worn to wasting

and decay is hungry, hasting:

in its death, i smell my own.

blood abandoned to be buried:

with its scent, the soil is sullied,

for the cat is called and carried

and the bird is broken bone.

\- DEAD BIRD IN THE GARDEN

4.

listen closely, bend your ear,

underneath the litter peer:

from the leafbed, pale and rot-fed,

rises tower quelled and queer.

there the spire weeps and wakes,

shaken by the footstep-quakes,

in its sorrow comes the

morrow -

sowing spires and fending

fear.

come, ye pilgrim, to the

tower

find the bones beneath its power,

ask the risen what was given

what lies buried under bower.

drink, ye thirsty, of the fountain

dripping from the dreadful mountain,

sup from dewspring, brimline curling,

underneath the shade's sharp shower.

- MUSHROOMS IN THE SHADE

5.

within the calm and cradled cup

of nestled leaves, whence insects sup,

you'll find the pool, the spring serene

filled up with waters clear and green.

come closer, friend, and gaze therein;

come see the

wonders held within.

approach, you're

weary: taste that

drink

and when you stand

upon the brink,

heed not the

warnings shrill and

stark

that ask what drink would seem so dark,

and why, if waters are so clear,

you cannot see what's lying here.

come drink, my fellow, thirsty friend,

for here cool succours never end.

come rest, come sleep, come deeper down

unto the edge, for you won't drown;

you're safe, you're weary, happy here,

so calm, be still, and come you near.

please come, my friend, down to the bank,

fret not about those past who drank.

\- CALL OF THE PITCHER-PLANT

6.

what use is such a net, too fine to catch

much more than drops of dew upon its thread?

and yet, and yet, how fine is such a net

thats purpose-made to catch the morning dew:

were i a weaver, poised with needle and a string,

could i so mythical a mesh entwine?

so simple is the craft that captures light,

as light is both the weaver's craft and aim.

how many days, how many nets were strung

that turned it from a trap into an art,

how many hunted creatures did it take

for function to become a work of art?

and yet, there hangs that web, all strung with dew,

an art that every morn is wrought anew.

- WEBS IN THE MORNING

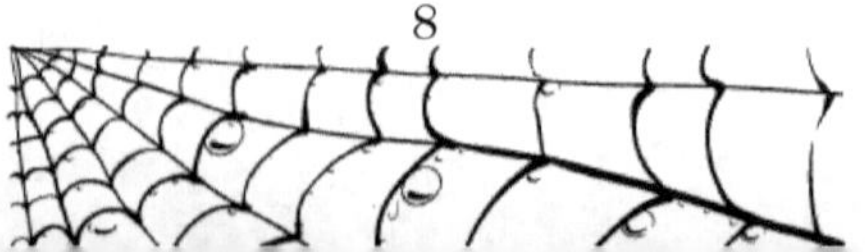

7.

softer than silence

come the wingbeats to their hall

swinging by gently

only sweet murmurs

betray the morning fellows

calling together

how loud is silence

when all are gone, and empty,

and absence a roar

\- BIRDS TO THE BIRDHOUSE

8.

by gleam of eye and clink of claw,

and bone-white teeth in gaping maw,

by curling tail and

blackest fur,

you'll know what

comes, the heinous

cur.

he comes for warmth, he comes for food,

we cannot keep him out for good.

he gives no peace, we give no rest

he's stubborn, our unwanted guest.

he makes his nest beneath the shelf,

he keeps his children by himself,

he finds the crumbs, we find the cat,

and rid ourselves from vermin rat.

\- RODENTS NESTING

9.

here we float amongst the starstream,

tiny specks of fragile daydream:

we're alone in void on all sides,

and too small to scream for aid.

so we drift in silence tolling,

lit up golden as we're falling.

glowing dust in endless cosmos

floating downward, all afraid.

- DUST IN SUNBEAMS

in a fragile eden

with its shining wall

is a verdant garden

and an arbor tall.

catch its maker gazing

in the morning light

for creation lazing

is a lovely sight.

there's a hundred creatures

that will call it home

happy with its features

and softly will roam.

a garden is a garden:

no matter what its size,

no matter if it darken,

no matter where it lies.

\- IVY IN A JAR

11.

oh, look - are you looking? - see them over
there?
they're gorging away with superior airs.
they've shoved off the needy, the weak, and the
poor
and their paying their homage to a fat, greedy
boor.
now, it's almost a mystery - to those who have
none -
why the fortunate hoard and belittle and shun,
but the truth is that kindness is something you
learn
and if you are given, you'll give too, in turn,
so if you've not wanted a day in your life,
you'll think nothing much of a stranger's hard
strife.
so the greedy will hoard, because they've no
cause,

and the needy will starve, 'cause those are the laws.

- PIGEONS IN MY GODDAMN BIRD FEEDER

i

go.

try

to go.

but am

halted.

stopped.

arrested.

by the wall

that stands

as a monument

to the sum of my

fettered, bound

disappointment.

- CAT AT THE DOOR

13.

Observation recorded:

///[function = almost_true]

if (on_looking, perspective_widens)

observe (microcosm)

let (sentence = "cities lie in the dust, forgotten

by their creators.")

return (question = "how can you empty a city in

a moment?")

return (whisper = "show me the sum of our

accomplishments.")

final (word = "ozymandias")

add_action ("look again")

[function: almost_true]///

- DUSTY MOTHERBOARDS

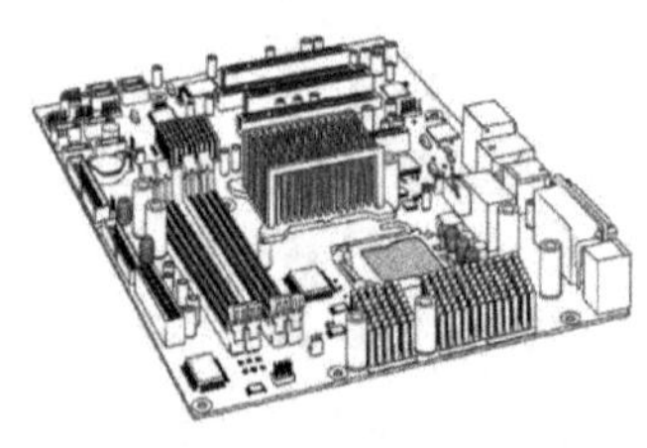

14.

magnitude beset

a relative frame

in frustration's guise.

sometimes i forget

that the sky's the same

no matter your size.

and ever i'll regret

whatever anger came

when i close my eyes.

- STEPPING ON A SPIDER

15.

i watched with hooded eyes the vast expanse

of powers twain, who glared each to the one

as interloper in their own domain.

the rage of tyrants faced by their own kind,

the howling cry of harrowed spite resounds,

for each themselves considers them supreme

and cannot suffer any challenger

to draw a breath within their sov'reign realm.

for each in envy lives for envy's sake

and seek to add their envy to their own.

the wind cares not, and rain ebbs not from them,

but fury needs a fertile ground to grow.

despite the wind, despite the raging storm,

they stand their ground, for anger is their form.

\- CATS ON A COLD TIN ROOF

hollowed pipes and paper towers,

corridors of sun-light echoes,

hidden hideous in flowers:

we are different than our fellows.

here we hang and here we hunger,

hear us murmur, we are coming:

hear us tear the air asunder,

hear the wings of war a-drumming.

if you've seen us, if you're near us,

you should know that it's too late.

there's no warning for your trespass:

meet our fury, meet your fate.

- WASPS' NEST

17.

How far did you fall

just to land

on me

did alter

your fate,

or was i your intended destination?

\- RAINDROPS ON A WINDOW

i'm a pilgrim in the desert

in a place that's most unpleasant

with no shelter and no succour

i'm one cheeky little f--

- ANT ON THE KITCHEN BENCH

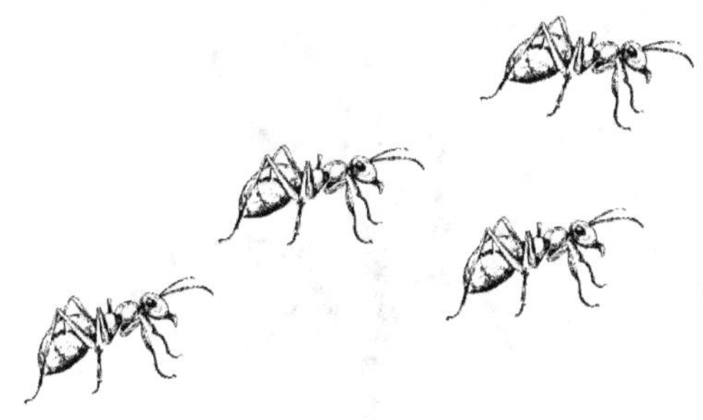

19.

made for the shadows

it was folly to dream of

surviving the day

\- FAINTED FUNGUS

20.

in the space between our thinking
is the largest world of all,
and unending void of hoping
microcosms we can't see.

the space behind the eyes
wars against the world before it,
every day is made a battle
'twixt what is and what could be.

- MICROCOSMS